And When I Deliver You... Change Your Clothes

by T.L. Goines

A Novel

This is a work of fiction created by the author. Names, characters, businesses, places, events, locales, and incidents are either the products of the author's imagination or used in a fictitious manner. Any resemblance to actual persons, living or dead, or actual events is purely coincidental

ISBN: 978-1-935256-80-9

L'Edge Press
P.O. Box 1652
Boone, NC 28607
ledgepress@gmail.com

Who is this book for? This book is for anyone who has experienced traumas in their life that no one knows about. This book is for the poor, middle class, educated, that woman who is functioning at the corporate level but at the same time bleeding like a wounded dog. This is for that person who smiles in front of the people but who cries when they are alone because they have not experienced total healing in their souls (mind, emotions, imaginations and memories).

This book is for the person who is tired of being told how they should function in their role in the home but is confused because the message is one-sided. And the young person who says

I am confused, I have been around, and I did not choose to be like this but because of a childhood trauma or because of a rape that occurred when I thought we were only playing at the time, what happened? Why? When I looked around and there was no Pop's (Father) to come to my rescue then I ...... [You fill in the blank reader].

Let's not forget the high level executive who has power but no family, money, but few trusted relationships, position but struggles with playing a role in the home because she fears that she will not be respected and has secretly said within 'I will never allow anyone to control me again or this time around I am looking out for me.'

May God deliver you from the opinions of people so that you can mature into what he has designed you to be and do what burdens you the most to make a positive change in your world.

—TG

Acknowledgements

First, I would like to acknowledge my wife of over 20 years. She has taught me so many lessons that I cannot name them all. If I would have to name something that she has taught me it would be I Corinthians 13 1-8. She is truly patient, kind, and someone who has a good heart. It is my pleasure to call her my wife. I know she loves me when sometimes it is hard for her to like me. I love you T.

Secondly, I would like to acknowledge my son and two daughters whom I love dearly. They have been my motivation in this project and I pray that this book will touch their lives and all who may see it. Although the culture around us may be changing I am proud to say that I have 'fathered' them and have not left them fatherless. Why do I say this? Because the impact or lack of Fathers in the life of children reaches beyond the scope of a person's life. One does not have to be perfect to be a father, only available to be a protector, guide, mentor, and influence when they are grown.

Finally, I would like to acknowledge my first Pastor (My Mother). Thank you for teaching me, encouraging me and setting a godly example for our family. I love you.

'Change your clothes define

In the Bible there is a story about a man who is moving his family from one location to a better location.

He had to move his family because his sons took revenge on men who had raped their sister. [Read the story in Genesis 34 –Message translation]

The story continues in Genesis 35 and in the latter part of verse 2 the father tells his family to "change your garments" Why would he say something like this? If you are leaving do you have time to do this? What difference does it make? We all have a past but sometimes negative residue from our past shows up in our present and negatively affects our world around us.

The act of changing one's clothes was intended to signify a repentant change of heart, that demonstrated a lifestyle that intentionally decided to leave a life without God and to embrace a new way of living that was centered on a biblical mindset of doing everything on a daily basis for the rest of your life. This is what Jesus meant when he told men whom he had taught according to Matthew 28: 19-20.

Because external gods (idols) were hidden beneath a carefully identified terebinth tree. Thus, paganism remained deeply rooted in the hearts of those in the home that embraced them causing an impact on the family but a comfort to the person who held on to them.

Let me define what a household idol meant to the culture of this family in Genesis.

Household idols: Laban spoke of them as his "gods" [Genesis 31:30]. These teraphim, small figurines of the family gods, held great meaning for the heirs. According to the ancient law around Haran, the sons, particularly the eldest, had the privilege of inheriting the family "gods," as well as all the property that went with them. Rachel stole them either to ridicule her father's religion (vv. 14-16), to lay claim to the inheritance, or to remain attached to her native religion, culture, or mindsets while embracing modern day secularism that was contrary to her faith to the true and living God. [Refence: Spirit Filled Life Bible, NKJ Version; copyright 1991]

The story to follow in this book will tell a modern day example of what this looks like.

Contact information of this writer

For speaking engagements, questions or comments write to:

goinestt@hotmail.com

Be sure to put the title of the book in the subject line. We will try to respond within 2-3 weeks. We ask that you be patient due to the nature of scheduling and other priorities.

Thank you,

Author

Author Jonetta Rose Barras explained to me the following facts that I did not realize could be so deep within. In her book, 'What ever happened to daddy's little girl' what happens to a little girl who grows up without a father? Can she ever feel truly loved and fully alive? Does she ever heal—or is she doomed to live a wounded, fragmented life and to pass her wounds down to her own children? Fatherlessness afflicts nearly half the households in America, and it has reached epidemic proportions in the African-American community, with especially devastating consequences for black women.

"We are legions—a choir of wounded—listen to the dirge we sing," writes Barras of the millions of black women like her who lost, either through abandonment, rejection, poverty, or death, the men who gave them life. A father is the first man in a girl's life—the first man to look in her eyes, protect her, care for her, love her unconditionally. Fathers fashion their daughters as expertly and as powerfully as they do their sons. When a girl loses this man, she grows up with an ache that nothing else can soothe. Psychologists have found that fatherless daughters are far more likely to suffer from debilitating rage, depression, abuse, and addictions; they tend to seek "sexual healing" through promiscuity or anti-intimate behavior and end up fearing or despising the men whose love they crave.

[Source: *Whatever Happened to Daddy's Little Girl?*: The Impact of Fatherlessness on Black Women by Jonetta Rose Barras; copyright 2000]

Whatever Happened to Daddy's Little Girl?

The Impact

Chapter 1

"Shaquan!", I could not do any better than you and you could not do any worse than me said her husband Andre. Andre had tried for years to love her the best way he could but in her mind, it was never enough. Andre always was the final blame for everything that went wrong in their lives, after all the preacher would tell them on Sunday morning that men were the heads of the homes. No one noticed how silent the church room became when this was echoed from the platform. The women cheered when the list of duties was read about the duties men should be doing in their homes. But Andre did not know that the speaker needed inner healing too. Instead of going to the source of all life the individual had suppressed feelings that were also deep, but they refused to acknowledge nor deal with them. Now they were affecting millions with their actions and the words that spewed out of their mouth from the platform. The doctors were perplexed why they could not find the root of their diagnoses or how it got started in the body.

Andre silently wondered to himself where he where he was missing it. He had suffered disrespect from his mother-n-law as his wife would sit in silence across the room when her mother would recall the foolishness of her ex-husband's past. Andre thought to himself, 'is not my wife supposed to respect her husband and not allow any women or man to disrespect him as the man of their house'? He was often compared to the other men at church and his wife would laugh and smiled with the other women at church but deep down she kept her distance and did not trust them out of her sight nor around her husband alone. Andre fell in love with Shaquan while they were dating and just after he asked her to marry him she became pregnant. Andre was happy when she broke the news to him that he was going to be a father but his soon to be mother-n-law was bitter and suspicious that her daughter was getting to have a man who would take care of her because she was pregnant.

Shaquan's mother was very bitter over her failed marriage to the man who broke her heart.

Andre was to embarrassed and ashamed to tell anyone what was going on in his home. Yelling and screaming, accusations about not being a supportive husband or servant leader who knew how to love his wife. What was he to do? Leave? Quit? Divorce or find a girlfriend on the side? As the months passed and Shaquan gave birth to her first child Andre was still unaware of what was to come in his future with his new bride. One thing he did know, and that was the commitment he made to himself to demonstrate love to her and to his child. Andre determined that he would not allow their child to be raised alone or by a pack of angry women who would over time commit 'emotional' incest with the child at the same time hating its father. This often reminded him of the scripture that said, 'one day women would say to men, I got my own home, car, career and money. Just give me your sperm (a child) and leave me alone, I don't need you anymore. But I will take your money if that is an option too.'

(author's paraphrase of Isaiah 4:1)

The Teenage Years

Chapter 2

As the years moved on their child (a son) grew and began to branch off to discover his own path in life. He was not a 'perfect' child (no one is) but he began to develop a dislike towards his father. Why? Because when he turned 12 years old he began to grow taller in height. It was during this time that his mother began to drop bitter words in his ears concerning her relationship with his father. She would began talking under her breath at times and as things like, 'don't be like him', he does not know how to treat a woman with respect because his dad was never around', and other damning phrases that tore down her home. Andre was unaware of this and thought that he had a loving relationship with her, after all she welcomed him sexually when he would arrive home after working 12-14 hours a day.

Andre thought that the change in his son's attitude change was due to fact that he was maturing and developing, he never suspected anything within his own home could be the cause of this demise that was happening.

[Note to the reader: If you are wondering Shaquan is an active church member and one day truly submitted her life to Jesus Christ at the altar]

What was wrong after 21 years of sitting in church? Was the Bible and its many stories only a placebo for a few hours on Sunday morning? Was it a big event to prepare for or just another theater where people gathered to be entertained by a man who would crack jokes, breath heavy (as if his asthma was bothering him) and not stop giving his presentation until all or half the people fainted? Andre believed in the power of God through the finished work on earth of Jesus Christ. He had personally experienced how God had kept him and his sibling through the ups and downs of the inner-city life he experienced. He personally experienced being raised by a single parent, a father and step-father who were partially involved in the home but loved him dearly. He thought of his brief relationship with his step-father often because he remembered that he was the one who cared for first before he knew his biological father and before his mother became pregnant from his seed. And he was a sinner who had grew up in the Roman Catholic church and had been molested by one of the Priest when he was a little boy. Although he would see his biological father periodically throughout the year. Andre had a brief reunion with his step-father returning into his life at the age of 17 only to lose him to a sudden death three years later.

Thank God for the former World War (II) veteran who came into his life while he was 5 years old. He and his siblings were mentored by he and his wife until their deaths and the birth of his son.

Andre found himself always trying to 'fix' the whining of his spouse but now came the time that he grew tired and had to decide about his own self-care and emotional survival. He began to question God. Why? If you are the God of miracles and source of all things, then why was Shaquan only experiencing 'crumbs' of what the church called deliverance and not total victory in this area of her life? Why he wondered. His heart would begin to beat fast in his chest when he would see her 'catch the spirit' in church (roll on the floor and cry) but cry for some unknown reason to him all the way home.

Was this to be his 'norm' in his marriage and life? To live with someone who lived life off their emotions which affected also their health, finances and relationships?

[Author's note: Now I don't want you to believe that Andre was 'perfect'. He wrestled with being the 'perfect' husband from others who were his peers.]

No one knew that Andre purposely submitted himself to the teachings (doctrine) of Jesus Christ that he had learned and continued to pursue as a man. Whenever the thoughts, ideas or suggestions would come Andre resisted the curses that had been spoken over him by others growing up regarding his future. What were they?

Spoken CURSES!!!!!

"YOU WILL HAVE AT LEAST 2-3 BABIES BY THE TIME YOU ARE 21 AND NOT TAKE RESPONSIBILITY FOR THEM AS AN UNWED FATHER

"YOU WILL HAVE AT LEAST ONE FELONY BY THE AGE OF 25"

"BY THE AGE OF 27 YOU WILL HAVE

CHILDREN BY MULTIPLE WOMEN"

Did this happen? No. By the time Andre reached his late 20s he experienced the birth of his first child, married to the love of his life and a bright future ahead of him.

Glory to God! His faith, trust and surrendering his life to God produced results and he was confused about his sexuality, masculinity or struggled with same-sex attractions.

Now what?

The Assignment

Chapter 3

Shaquan and Andre sat in church again on a beautiful sunny day in May. The assignment that was given from the minister who had been invited to speak for three days was an application to scripture that Andre had never heard of. He challenged everyone to go home and write down for 65 days what they were grateful for what they complained about the most. They were required to diligently take 7-10 minutes per day and begin to list the two items on a sheet pf paper, keep a running log of this for the next 65 days. The second part of the assignment required that they memorize 2 -4 scripture verse that were related to this area of their life. Each day they were to answer the following questions after reading and memorizing the related verses:

- What does God's word say?
- What does God's word mean?
- What does God's word mean to me?
- What will I do to live it out in my life?
- What is something I learned today and how will it change what you do tomorrow?
- What can I do tomorrow to show that I have learned and applied something new?

The assignment was to be done for the next 65 days. Little did they know what was about to take place in their lives. This journey would take discipline (something that Andre did when he arose faithfully ever morning to do workouts at the gym come rain or shine) and commitment (something Shaquan would do when she would sit patiently for 2-3 hours to get her hair done). Andre knew he had to fight against the laziness and norm of 'church as usual without application' that he had fallen into. He could some quote verses but understanding how to properly apply them fell short. He had not learned how to bridge the gap he had between his knowledge with the application and wisdom of the scriptures.

At the end of the sermon the preacher shared the story of a coupled that he had counseled who refused to do the application assignment(s) that he would give them. When he would meet with them and inquire about their results of their 'homework' he would be met with excuses and inertia stares back at him. It did not surprise him since they refused to do the work that they experience little to no results in their personal lives nor relationships.

Before sitting down that day the preacher told the congregation the following allegory which Andre could not get out of his mind:

'There was a girl named Rosa who had broken up with Jose after 10 months. They met each other 'one casual sex Friday' night at the club on Friday night before going to their perspective churches to participate in the choir sing-off. They both felt that this weekly activity was fine because when asked if this was contrary to what their bibles taught the would say, "this does not make anyone a slut, cause when you can't remember it, it doesn't count!

Rosa told Jose that she did not want to see him anymore and that the problem was not him, but her. "I need time to heal", she said.

After six months Rosa contacted Jose, out of the blue, she wrote him a txt.

'Jose, I was wrong and made a mistake, I blamed you

For my car being vandalized and I was wrong. I want you back.'

PS 'Congratulations on winning the lottery!'

Funny how willing and able people can do things when there is a personal benefit attached!

I Don't Want the Process–Just Give Me What I Want

Chapter 4

Andre arose up early as he usually did, he heard an inner voice say to him, "today will you change your mindset, exercise self-discipline and be teachable to everything that I will show you"? You will change if you, listen without judgment, do not judge or attempt to fix anything, just listen with your ears, eyes and mind. Andre immediately began redesigning his thoughts, critically evaluating what he was thinking, observing how his words aligned with his daily actions in relation to others and himself and what he spoke. For example, he noticed that he would sit and watch videos regarding nutrition and exercise and then jump up and rush out to buy products and food. However, after 3 months his excitement had weaned, and he was surrounded by the dusty product(s) he had purchased and the dates on the 'healthy food' had expired or spoiled. This time he had to consciously and intentionally, on purpose in a careful and unhurried way pay attention to what thoughts ran through his mind, what he spoke. He practiced doing self-reflecting and self-regulatory on himself. Everything depended on what he decided to think about.

As the days went on and Andre began to apply the steps day by day and principles to his everyday life he started to notice things about himself that he never saw. He discovered that he had stopped 'announcing' to everyone what he was going to do, he just did it. Following the instructions that he heard that morning also allowed him to understand and see his mindset more clearly. He recognized Shaquan's mindset more clearly and why their relationship struggled in their everyday lives as tongue-talking, Bible quoting, church goers, choir singing members on Sunday morning. Andre began to ask God in prayer everyday how he could see past the 'blinders' that he had in his life. He wrote down 2-3 mindsets that he had recognized in his life and began to replace them with relevant bible verses that he looked up on his phone. He went out and purchased a bible dictionary to gain a deeper and richer understanding of the what the words meant so he could properly get the entire picture of the stories that he read.

For example, he read the story about King David's son Adonijah and discovered how David's wife Bathsheba had promoted her son Solomon to succeed him while David was at a weak moment in his life and mainly forgetful in this thinking during his dying days. This example helped Andre to see that this same act had occurred in his own family when he was a young adult and his grandmother manipulated him to hold a private bank account for her so that she could keep money hidden from her husband. Although he was told why (grandma became bitter that grandpa 12 years earlier because he spent money on an investment that she did not approve). He was not aware that her bitterness towards him had grew inside over many years because she had resented a family decision he had made. Although she did not agree with the decision at that time, as the years went by bitterness, and rejection coupled with her already low self-esteemed and actions set loose an unhealthy relationship with him and between her children after her death. The children barley bonded or spoke to one another anymore.

Andre noticed that this same or similar dysfunction had slowly began creeping into his thoughts. What's wrong with having secrets he thought? The thought came to his mind (and almost out of his mouth) that witch Shaquan only cares about what benefits her. If the rent is paid, she has a roof over her head, food to eat, she is just leeching off me as her 401K retirement blanket.

An occasional 'casual sex' encounter (casual sex with him/her because I need sexual gratification and nothing more) with a good piece of meat in the bedroom is how she operated in the marriage.

Although his thoughts were real he intentionally chose to take a different mindset path towards his wife. First, he prayed specifically that God would remove blinders from her mind so that she would change destructive habits that were ruining their marriage, he also got involved himself with other people and communities who did not have the same dysfunction as he had, and he began to grow as he did this on a regular basis. He was showed by an elder in the group that God held him accountable for how he responded to his wife whether she did the right the thing or not. He was shown the scripture Isaiah 59:1 (Common English Bible translation) which read 'Look! The Lord does not lack the power to save, nor are his ears too dull to hear, but your misdeeds have separated you from your God. Your sins have hidden his face from you so that you aren't heard' and Proverbs 27:17 (Good News Translation), which read 'People learn from one another, just as iron sharpens iron.'

This new lifestyle and revelation not only inspired the information he received, in addition he was seeing his own eyes transformation from the impartation of wisdom from others. Andre recalled from his notes that he wrote down how growth could not take place if he did not apply what he heard and he if continued to start and stop during his journey. Why stop applying this in this area only, he thought? It was not enough to listen, laugh, cry and hug people but application and continual application would bring transformation and life changing results.

The scriptures were working in his life!

Will this Church Thing work at the Bar-B-Que this Weekend?

Chapter 5

This new thing that Andre was experiencing started to affect his health, relationship and finances. Now he wondered if he would be able to influence his family at the family reunion. Normally his uncles would start off drinking and end up fighting one another before the sun went down. His aunt's would start maliciously gossiping about how their husbands treated them and some would even say that they had never encountered a good man other than their daddy or their son or grandson's in their life. He really was not in the mood to hear the elders in the family rehash how they were still angry with one another because of something that occurred when they were 12-year-old and now they were in their 80s.

Andre wondered if it was possible for a holy respect for God could happen with his family? It would take a bit of optimism to believe that God's presence of peace and harmony would fall on them let alone to the partying heathens in his family nevertheless, he prayed and asked the Lord about this.

Immediately he was impressed to read the story of Jonah, and study it diligently before he left home. As he read and observed the outrageous and incredibly humorous behavior of the sailors who never had any connection to the God of Israel nor any of His people like Jonah, till they had the misfortune to be on the ship where a disobedient Hebrew prophet had purchased a ticket as a paying passenger, and the near-death experience this caused for everyone on the ship scared the living daylights out of these men. Eventually their misfortune turned into the greatest fortune of all when they came to revere and worship the God of Israel. Wow! This answered his question. Yes! It is possible, and it can happen again Andre said.

As Andre continued to study the story and discuss what he had read with his accountability mentor and Christian brother Joe whom he trusted and did not see as a 'Pope figure' but as a biblical student in this journey of life Andre learned that even though the harrowing story of Jonah on the ship is well known, the emphasis mainly was placed on the fish that the Lord prepared to swallow up Jonah.

Andre learned that observing the passage and reading the passage multiple times in multiple translations brought new light on his study.

He was seeing by the Spirit of God within himself that this story was applicable to everyday living and how trusting God in obedience could be applied in his life. He never thought to ask the Holy Spirit to help him in situations before because his dependence and confidence was normally in himself first and his money.

As he read the passage with precision

and for detail he saw that the Lord sent an extraordinary storm so that these experienced sailors were terrified and at their wits' end.

Andre notice that instead of pounding Jonah into a pulp, they asked him who he was, where he was from, what his nationality was, what his livelihood was, and who his people were (his ethnicity). Andre also saw how God had everyone on that boat right where He wanted them! They had seen the awesome, miraculous power of Jonah's God. Andre saw in the details of the story how the respect of the Lord CAN and DOES fall on the unsaved.

At that moment he prayed for his family, their children and friends who were coming to the family reunion. By praying for their salvation, he was trusting God to:

- shorten the time till they find the Lord and repent
- make the storm less brutal at the upcoming bar-b-que for everyone

Andre learned when he studied his Bible and read it repeatedly, for the details and for insight that the text began to speak to him louder than he could stand.

The Miseducation of a Happy but Untaught Church Goer in this Present Day

Chapter 6

After several years and months of following this one principle Andre wrote in his journal the following life lessons that he learned—Reflections…

They say if you tell me I may forget,

Teach me and I may remember,

Involve me and I change, as

I apply what I have learned I become

For I have learned that tell'n me

Ain't training and experience is

Not the best teacher. Yes, experience is a teacher

But not necessarily the best. However, it

Is a school that a stubborn fool will defiantly attend,

For the worse thing a parent can do to their child is

Stand by in silence while they dishonor God's

Set order in the home. This allows the enemy to

Mock God's divine order. This I am sure God

Will let things keep getting worse until I get the

Message. God will cause distress to

get me to come

Nearer to Him. (Ask Mr. Jonah in the Bible about his experience)

God is waiting on us

Poem -2-

I AM STILL LEARNING..

To be patient with others and not to
move in anger. Every day I am

Preparing for my future and my obe-
dience or laziness to biblical principles
will determine the outcome for me, if
I continue to add to what I am hoping
for I shall suceed

And be fruitful

I will be known as a 'baller' or 'shot
caller' so that my faith is not trusting

In my morals chiefly but is a demon-
stration of what my God has

Promised me. Now what characteristics & actions will I add today? Hmm...

- goodness towards myself and others
- knowledge that pertains to my spirit, soul and body so that I may be balanced in my daily living
- self-control over my mouth, habits, body, passions etc.
- perseverance
- godliness, intentionally allowing God to be involved in every area of my

life and not lowering our relationship to a two-hour session on Sunday

and maybe a 40-minute bible study but I go away and

worship my TV, iPhone with my full attention for

40 hours or more

- Brotherly kindness by valuing others no Andreer their status,

Ethnicity, age, social class or occupation and

- Unconditional love, I have not use of childish games towards others at my age.

I have learned from the words of my father when he said to me:

"son if you don't take heed and hear me now, you will feel me later

When I am not present"

I have learned that he was correct because I 'feel him' and hear his wisdom now.

Because my rejection of his instruction has affected my finances, health and relationships in the past

I have come to understand in my Christian relationship that

I don't have any trouble, all I need to do is apply my faith in God

Counseling a Different Approach

The Counseling Session Trisha and Billy

Chapter 7

Trisha and Billy walked into the office and sat down in front of the biblical counselor because Trisha felt that her marriage was failing, and Billy was ready to leave with the divorce papers in his hand after 7 years of marriage and five years of hell in the marriage. Trisha began by explaining to the counselor that she was a Christian and wanted to save her marriage, she sobbed as she told the counselor that

Billy was a kind man and a good provider but that he seemed to not take her seriously and would not allow her to voice her feelings when she would sometimes raise her voice during an intense conversation. Billy would abruptly say, 'I need to leave right now' and then walk away'. Trisha felt down on herself and just wanted him to stop. 'If he would just become a Christian, she said we would not have these problems, I feel more connected to our 4 children than I do to him and since they have all left home I don't know what I am going to do'. Billy immediate turned and ask the counselor, 'are you a Christian too?' Yes, replied the counselor. Is that a problem? Yes, replied Billy, 'I told my wife that I would agree to go to counseling if she did not bring me to a Christian counselor'. Billy began ranting and raving for the next 5 minutes how he would never trust his wife again.

When the counselor heard this he immediately turned to Trisha and began to ask:

Counselor: Trisha, is this true?

Trisha: Yes, he did say that

Counselor: Why did you deceive him by lying to him about this meeting today?

Trisha: Because I want him to be a Christian and start going to church

Counselor: Trisha do you know that the scriptures tell us not to lie or be deceitful to our spouses or one another?

Trisha: Yes, but I thought that this time he would change his mind if we came to you

Counselor: Have you read in your bible (Gen. 20:9-11) where it reads; Then Abimelech called Abraham and said to him, "What have you done to us? And how have I sinned against you that you have brought on me and on my kingdom a great sin? You have done to me things that ought not to be done." And Abimelech said to Abraham, "What have you encountered, that you have done this thing?" Abraham said, "Because I thought, surely there is no fear of God in this place, and they will kill me because of my wife" or (Isa. 59:2-3) But your iniquities have made a separation between you and your God, and your sins have hidden His face from you so that He does not hear. For your hands are defiled with blood and your fingers with iniquity; your lips have spoken falsehood, your tongue mutters wickedness. Or Good News Translation

(GNT) (Isa. 59:2-4 MSG) 'It is because of your sins that he doesn't hear you. It is your sins that separate you from God when you try to worship him. You are guilty of lying, violence, and murder.' You go to court, but you do not have justice on your side. You depend on lies to win your case. You carry out your plans to hurt others.

Lying is a cause of unanswered prayer. Are you aware of that? You are sinning against your own marriage to get what you want.

At this time Billy calmed down and began to listen to the counselor talk to Trisha and began to say, 'tell her reverend! You are right! The counselor ended the session and advised that Trisha return home, repent to her husband and to continue to pray for him treating him as if he were already a believer in the eyes of God. He advised her that if she continued to do this as a lifestyle that God would honor her faith, but he could not tell her when Billy would surrender his life to God. If he is not asking you to sin, honor him.

Billy heard the conversation and was silent. Three years later he returned to the counselor's office unknowingly to Trisha to ask what this new Christian life thing was about. The counselor shared with Billy in more detail the seriousness of the decision that he was about to make. Although things were somewhat better he asked for more help between him and Trish.

Don & Doris

Chapter 8

Don and Doris marriage had started 7 years ago and although nothing happened on their wedding night (they slept in separate rooms) Don wondered what was going on and was ready to leave. He was angry with God and was depressed over choosing Doris to be his bride. He felt angry and was embarrassed to reveal to the ecclesiastical leadership at his church his dilemma.

Although they had a short courtship Don could not understand why his wife decided to up and quit her job three weeks after the wedding. When he would express his concerns with her she would say, 'according to the Bible you are supposed to love me, care for me and be the head.' Yes, he would reply however, 'but you never said that you did not want to work before I put a ring on your finger,' and besides you don't believe you should cook or engage in intimacy with him. Don was unaware that his beloved had been previously raped 3 years before they met each other, and she would have flash backs of her attacker when Don would approach her in the bedroom. Don confessed to the counselor that he was wrong for sleeping with another woman after being married for six years without any sexual relations with Doris and he was truly repentant when he confessed to her.

After several weeks of confronting Doris with the scriptures concerning her martial relationship she confessed about the trauma she had experienced prior to meeting Don. Although her family was aware of the incident that had occurred they vowed to keep this as their family secret.

When Don was made aware of what had happened to Doris and the years of secrets, silence and excuses he had endured he excused himself from the counseling session to go to the bath-room and never returned.

Andre & Shaquan

Final Session

Chapter 9

It was day sixty-six and the exercise that Andre and Shaquan were challenged to complete was over. Andre shared with his wife over the sixty-six days the insights, blessings and the things that he had learned about himself. Andre had even decided that he wanted to help others at the church who were struggling. When it came time for Shaquan to share she said, 'oh I forgot about that' it was good in theory, but that exercise is not really reality to me.'

Andre listened intently and ask the counselor what his thoughts were concerning their experience and what he was to do since his wife refused to take the exercise seriously. The counselor advise that he had no control over what Shaquan would or would not do with the message that she heard. He should continue to love her and not allow the frustration of her secret 'sins' to frustrate him, 'God will have to be the final authority in your relationship. Trust him.'

Andre sat in silence and Shaquan stared coldly at the counselor. The silence was deafening, and Shaquan wondered what Andre was thinking.

Andre finally broke his silence and said, starting now, I forgive those who've hurt me in the past and peacefully detach from them. I am worth moving forward!"

Shaquan began to cry bitterly. The counselor turned to Shaquan and ask are you willing to know do the assignment for the good and benefit of your marriage?

The End

[Now I asked **YOU** which lifestyle are you imitating in the stories of this book and when will you intentionally and continually change with the help of God?

Do you just read your Bible daily or are you allowing the message to read your life? Thank God that he always loves and corrects us with His truth and grace.]

CPSIA information can be obtained
at www.ICGtesting.com
Printed in the USA
BVHW092326290519
549652BV00005B/28/P

9 781935 256809